WHO'S iN tHe tRee tHat SHOULDN'T Be?

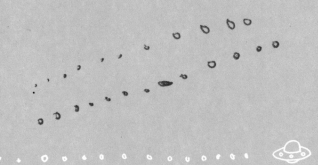

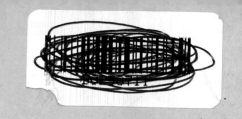

For Sophie and our daughter Ellie

A TEMPLAR BOOK

First published in the UK in 2014 by Templar Publishing
 an imprint of The Templar Company Limited,
Deepdene Lodge, Deepdene Avenue, Dorking, Surrey, RH5 4AT, UK
www.templarco.co.uk

ISBN 978-1-84877-613-5 (hardback)
ISBN 978-1-84877-614-2 (paperback)

Edited by Libby Hamilton

Printed in China

WHO'S IN THE TREE THAT SHOULDN'T BE?

CRAIG SHUTTLEWOOD

templar publishing

WHO'S iN THE **tReE** THAT SHOULDN'T BE? LET'S LifT THE FLAP AND WE WiLL **See!**

WHO DOES NOT **BELONG** IN GRASS SO LONG, WITH BiG ROUND HEAD AND ARMS SO **STRONG?**

WHO
IN THE **AIR**
SHOULD NOT BE THERE,
WITH FUNNY NOSE
AND HEAD SO **BARE?**

IN THE DESERT **DROUGHT**,
WHO'S THE ODD ONE OUT,
WITH CURLY TAIL
AND SNUFFLY **SNOUT?**

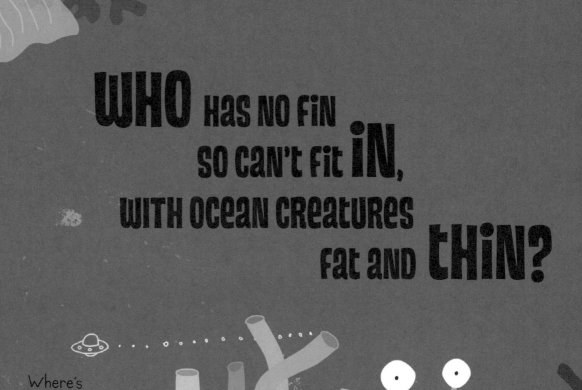

WHO HAS NO FIN SO CAN'T FIT **IN**, WITH OCEAN CREATURES FAT AND **THIN?**

Where's my twin?

Nice beaky grin!

IN ICE AND SNOW
WHO DOES NOT GO,
WITH MANE SO THICK
AND ROAR SO LOW?

ZOO

WHO IN DEEP SPACE IS OUT OF PLACE, IS OUT OF PLACE, WITH LONG, THIN NECK AND STARTLED FACE?

Do you want to race?

Back to base?

This place is ace!

ZOO

WHO'S IN THIS ZOO
AND JUST WON'T DO?

DID YOU GUESS THE NAMES OF ALL THE ANIMALS?

Giraffe

Peacock

Lion

(Bird)